PEGASUS ENCYCLOPEDIA LIBRARY

Experiments and Activities
GENERAL SCIENCE

Edited by: Aparna Chatterji
Managing editor: Tapasi De
Designed by: Vijesh Chahal and Anil Kumar
Illustrated by: Suman S. Roy, Tanoy Choudhury
Colouring done by: Vinay Kumar, Sonu, Kiran Kumari & Pradeep Kumar

GENERAL SCIENCE

CONTENTS

Introduction 3
Underwater fountain 4
Erupting volcano 5
Invisible letter 6
Red cabbage, the indicator 7
Misleading depths 8
Aerodynamic paradox 9
Blowing a paper ball into a bottle 10
Water mountain 11
Water roses 12
Balancing 13
Humpty Dumpty that never falls 14
Flying apart 15
Watery merry-go-round 16
Bottle on a bottle 17
Speed of water 18
Air scales 19
How to cheat a scale 20
How to make a rainbow 21
A mini-cinema 22
Kaleidoscope 23
Misled by water 24
Water as a lens 25
A Balancing Caper 26
Push at a distance 27
Energy changes 28
Self-adhesive ice 29
The jumping coin 30
Index 32

Introduction

Learning and experiencing new things is a continuous process. Children are much more inquisitive than we elders are. They are always bubbling with enthusiasm when it comes to knowing new things. That is the reason they are so full of questions. This enthusiasm should never be curbed; instead, it should be encouraged!

It is a proven fact that children learn the most by doing, experiencing and seeing things. Teaching them through books and worksheets only, does not suffice. We all know that 'seeing is believing'.

But sometimes due to the constraint of time and many other factors, elders are not successful in giving those experiences and exposure to their children which they deserve.

Here is an encyclopedia based on General Science which is full of simple activities and experiments which the children can do by themselves. It will definitely help them to develop a rational frame of mind and also sharpen their power of reasoning.

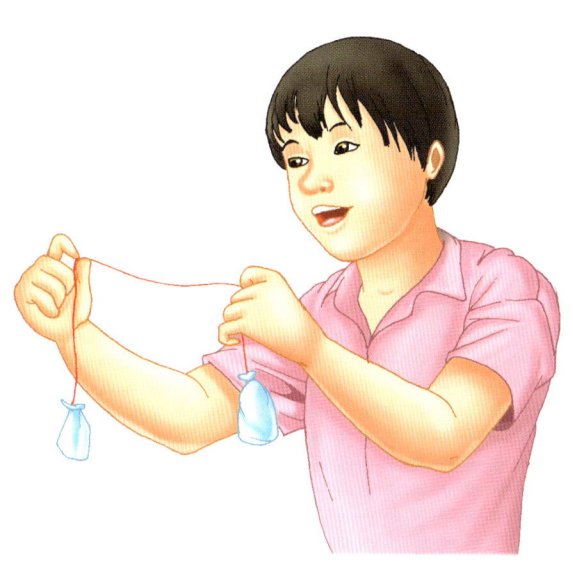

GENERAL SCIENCE

Underwater fountain

The fact

The same liquid has different densities at different temperatures. This experiment will prove it.

What you need

- A large glass vessel filled with water
- A small glass vessel with a stopper
- Some ink

How to do the experiment?

1. Pour cold water into the large vessel.
2. Pour hot water into the small vessel, add a few drops of ink, close it and shake.
3. Place the small vessel at the bottom of the large one.
4. Remove the small vessel's stopper.

What will happen?

The warm coloured water will rise and stay on top of the cool water. After some time, the coloured and clear waters will mix.

Astonishing fact

Did you know that there is the same amount of water in the world today as when the earth was first created? The earth will not gain or lose any water because it is recycled by nature.

Conclusion

The molecules of the hot water move faster than those of the cold water. The hot water is therefore less dense and also lighter; so it tends to climb up. Once their temperatures are equalised, the coloured water will sink and mix with the clear water.

Erupting volcano

The fact

Carbon dioxide is the gas which makes carbonated drinks so fizzy. If you shake a bottle of soda and then quickly open the bottle, the gas inside bubbles and rushes out of the bottle. Carbon dioxide is also useful for other things. It is used in fire-extinguishers and also helps cakes to rise. In this experiment you will be able to form carbon dioxide bubbles.

What you need

- A small glass jar
- A saucer
- Plasticine
- Bicarbonate of soda
- Vinegar

- Red food dye
- A teaspoon

How to do the experiment?

1. Place the jar in the middle of the saucer.
2. Cover its sides with plasticine to make the shape of a volcano cone.
3. Carefully fill half the jar with bicarbonate of soda.
4. Add some red food dye to it.
5. Using the spoon, slowly pour vinegar into the soda.
6. Stand back and observe.

What will happen?

Bubbles will form in the mixture and flow over the sides of the volcano.

Conclusion

The mixture of acetic acid in the vinegar and bicarbonate of soda form bubbles of carbondioxide gas. The bubbles are light and immediately rise to the surface, and the mixture begins to foam. The foam rises and flows over the sides, just like lava in a volcano.

GENERAL SCIENCE

Invisible letter

The fact

It is possible to write a message which no one will be able to read unless you want them to. Let us see how to do this through this experiment.

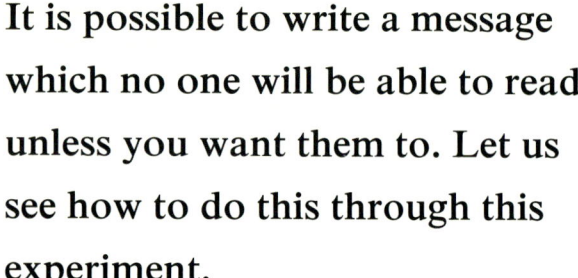

What you need

- A toothpick
- Some vinegar or lemon juice
- Paper
- A candle
- Match box

How to do the experiment?

1. Break the toothpick into half and use the thicker end as a pen.
2. Dip it into vinegar or lemon juice and write a message on the paper.
3. Wait until the paper dries.
4. Light the candle and carefully hold the paper close to the flame.

What will happen?

After the message on the paper dries, it will disappear. But heating it on the flame will bring up the writing again.

What did you learn?

Once the 'ink' evaporates from the paper, the writing will not be visible. When this paper is exposed to heat, the parts which had held the 'ink' react with oxygen at a lower temperature than the rest of the paper, which makes them darker and brings up the message on the paper.

Red cabbage, the indicator

The fact

Red cabbage juice contains a pigment called flavin. Very acidic solutions turn flavin red in colour while basic solutions turn it green.

What you need

- Half red cabbage
- A pot of water
- A knife
- A cutting board
- Paper napkins or filter paper
- Lemon juice, vinegar and liquid soap

How to do the experiment?

1. Ask an adult to slice up the cabbage. Boil it in water for about five minutes.
2. Take the cabbage out of the water and let the water cool. Cut the paper napkins or filter paper into ribbons.
3. Dip the ribbons into the water. Let the ribbons soak.
4. Dry the ribbons. After they are dry, drip on them drops of vinegar, lemon juice and liquid soap

What will happen?

The stains on the ribbons will be of different colours.

Note: An important indicator often used by scientists is litmus.

Conclusion

Red cabbage contains a chemical which we call an indicator. Indicators change colour when you add to them acids or bases. The juice of the red cabbage turns green when it is combined with a base (for example bicarbonate of soda) and turns red again when an acid is added (for example vinegar). Instead of the cabbage you can also use the petals of sanicle, which also contain an indicator that changes colours when acids or bases are added.

Misleading depths

The fact

When light moves from one medium to another, it bends. This phenomenon is known as refraction of light. Refraction can produce strange visual effects. Let us see how.

What you need

- A glass jar
- A coin
- Water
- Cardboard

The Fact

Seas, lakes and rivers often appear less deep than they really are because refraction makes the bottom seem nearer. Fishermen, who use harpoons, never aim at the fish where their eyes see them but at a point which seems lower in water.

How to do the experiment?

1. Make a cardboard shield as shown.
2. Put the coin in the jar and put the shield in front of the jar.
3. Position yourself so you can see the top of the jar, but not the coin.
4. Tell a friend of yours to slowly pour water into the jar.

What will happen?

As water fills the jar, the coin will gradually appear on the water surface!

Conclusion

The coin has become visible due to the refraction of rays of light. On pouring water into the jar, refraction of light takes place. As a result, the coin appears to be placed at a position that is higher than its actual position. Thus, it becomes visible.

Aerodynamic paradox

The fact

Wind forces the branches of trees to bend in the direction in which it is blowing. But airstreams can also move objects in completely unexpected directions. Let us see how.

A step further

You can see the same paradox in action if you try to blow a ping-pong ball out of a funnel by blowing hard through it.

Note: we call everything that happens contrary to what can be expected a 'paradox'.

What you need

- Two pencils
- Two pieces of thin paper

How to do the experiment?

1. Hold the two pieces of paper on the pencils as shown.
2. Now blow hard between them.

What will happen?

Instead of being blown apart as you expected, the sheets will cling to each other!

Conclusion

By blowing between the two paper strips, you cause the air between the strips to move. This lessens the air pressure between the strips. On the other hand, the air pressure on the outer sides of the strips remains high which forces the strips inwards as it pushes them towards the area of lower pressure.

Blowing a paper ball into a bottle

The fact

Air pressure can move objects. Let us see how.

What you need

- An empty bottle
- A small paper ball

How to do the experiment?

1. Lay the bottle on the table horizontally.
2. Put the ball of paper in the neck of the bottle and try to blow it inside.

What will happen?

Instead of flying in, the ball will hit you in the face!

What did you learn?

The air that you blew into the bottle goes past the paper ball and hits the back or bottom of the bottle. This increases the air pressure inside the bottle. As the compressed air rushes out, it carries the paper ball out with it.

Conclusion

Air moves from a region of high pressure to a region of low pressure.

Water mountain

The fact

It is quite amazing how many coins we can drop into a full glass of water without making it spill over the brim. Let us see how, through this experiment.

What will happen?

The water level will rise, but it will still not spill over.

What you need

- A glass of water
- Metal coins

How to do the experiment?

1. Fill the glass with water up to the very brim.
2. Put coins into the water carefully, one by one.

Conclusion

We can observe a phenomenon called surface tension. Water molecules on the surface are exposed to the action of molecular forces towards the interior of the water. They make the surface act like a stretched rubber membrane, preventing the water from spilling over.

GENERAL SCIENCE

Water roses

The fact

Absorption of water by capillaries causes them to swell and become turgid.

4. Sprinkle a few drops of water on the paper flowers.

What will happen?

The petals will open slowly.

What you need

- Smooth paper
- A pencil
- Scissors
- A vessel with water

How to do the experiment?

1. Cut out paper flowers as shown.
2. Colour and fold the petals inwards.
3. Float the paper flowers in the vessel of water.

Conclusion

Paper is made mainly of plant fibres which contain tiny tubes (capillaries). As the water enters the capillaries, the paper slowly swells and the petals slowly open.

12

Balancing

The fact

The centre of gravity is that point in an object where there is as much weight on one side as on the other. When we locate the centre of gravity in an object we can get that object to balance.

What you need

- An unopened bottle
- A cork stopper
- A needle
- Two forks

How to do the experiment?

1. Carefully stick the needle into the cork, then stick the two forks into opposite sides of the cork as shown. Balance the other end of the needle on the cap of the bottle carefully until the whole set up stands in a state of equilibrium.

A step further

Balance a ruler on a pencil held horizontally. Place various objects on the ruler's ends (erasers, sharpeners etc.). To preserve the balance, the position of the pencil will always have to be nearer the heavier of the two objects.

Conclusion

By adjusting the angle and location of the forks you can make the needle stand straight up. The needle balances because of the fact that there is exactly as much weight on one side of the needle as on the other side. The point of the needle is the centre of gravity.

GENERAL SCIENCE

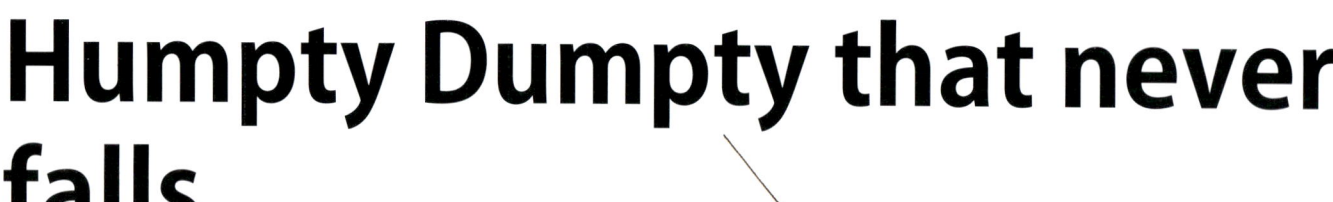

Humpty Dumpty that never falls

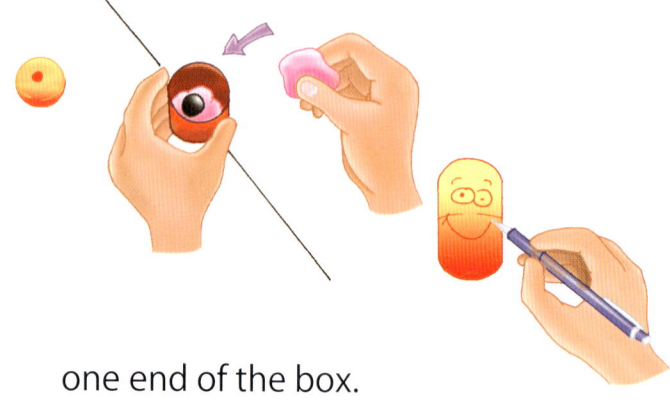

The fact

Objects always tend to assume the most stable position possible. The lower their centre of gravity, the easier it is for them to return to a state of equilibrium. In this experiment, you can make a Humpty Dumpty who will show you this rule.

What you need

- A plastic box from the chocolate egg surprise
- A metal ball
- Plasticine
- A felt-tipped pen

How to do the experiment?

1. Fix the metal ball with the plasticine at one end of the box.
2. Close the box and draw a face on it.

What will happen?

In whichever way you move the Humpty Dumpty, it will always bounce back to the same vertical position.

Conclusion

The weight of the plasticine makes the centre of gravity of the ball occur just below the point where it touches the ground. This makes Humpty Dumpty balance and bounce back to the same vertical position.

Flying apart

The fact

Every action has an equal and opposite reaction.

What you need

- An empty matchbox
- Matches
- A razor blade
- Thread

How to do the experiment?

1. Use the thread to tie the razor blade around the box as shown.
2. Hang the box with another piece of thread as shown.
3. Break the thread holding the razor blade by burning it with a glowing matchstick.

What will happen?

The razor blade will fly to one side (action) and the box to the other (reaction).

Conclusion

As the razor blade flies to one side it exerts an equal and opposite force on the box which then moves or flies off to the opposite side.

Watery merry-go-round

The fact

Every action has an equal and opposite reaction.

What you need

- A small plastic bottle
- Two plastic tubes
- Some string

How to do the experiment?

1. Bend the tubes, pierce the bottle and insert the tubes into the bottle. Then hang the bottle, as shown in the picture.
2. Fill the bottle with water.

What will happen?

Water will flow through the tubes and the bottle will begin to turn in a direction opposite to that of the flow of water.

Conclusion

As the water begins to flow through the tubes in a particular direction (action), the bottle begins to turn in an opposite direction (reaction).

Bottle on a bottle

The fact

Inertia tends to keep motionless objects where they are. To get things moving you have to overcome inertia of rest. In other words, "A body at rest tends to remain at rest."

What you need

- Two bottles of glass
- A piece of thin cardboard

How to do the experiment?

1. Place the bottles on top of each other with the cardboard between them as shown.
2. Pull away the cardboard sharply.

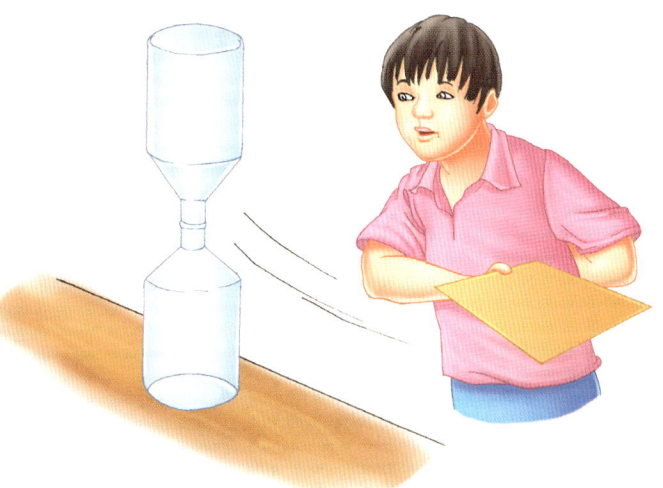

What will happen?

The upper bottle will retain its state of rest.

Warning!

Quite a lot of skill is needed for performing this trick. You can practice for it by surrounding the bottom bottle with pillows so the top one doesn't break if it falls.

Conclusion

The bottle on the top remains standing still as inertia tends to keep it that way. The card snaps away so quickly that the bottle on the top has no chance to follow the card. Gravity pulls it down on the bottle at the bottom.

17

GENERAL SCIENCE

Speed of water

The fact

We know what speed is from our everyday life. If objects traverse different paths in the same period of time, we say that their speeds differ. How can we determine the speed at which water flows in a river?

What you need

- Two wooden pegs
- A piece of wood
- A stopwatch or watch having a second hand

How to do the experiment?

1. Fix the pegs on the river bank. They will be your objects of reference.
2. Measure the distance between the pegs.
3. Throw the piece of wood into the river and see how long it takes it to pass from one peg to the other.
4. Divide the distance by the time elapsed. You will get a figure showing the speed, to which, add the unit of measurement (metres per second or m/s).

A step further

You can measure the speed of an electric train in the same manner, if you know the distance between the poles carrying the wire feed.

Conclusion

Speed is defined as the distance covered by an object per unit time.
Mathematically, speed=Distance/Time

Air scales

The fact

We know that hot air is lighter than cold air.

What you need

- An old ruler
- Two plastic cups
- Three pieces of string
- A candle
- Matches
- Scissors
- A drill

How to do the experiment?

1. Drill three holes on the ruler, one in the middle and the others near the ends at an equal distance from the middle.
2. Suspend the cups at the ends as shown in the picture.
3. Suspend the whole set up as shown and balance it.
4. Light the candle and place it under the cup suspended upside-down

What will happen?

The side of the ruler with the candle will go upwards.

Conclusion

As it is heated by the candle, the air in the cup expands and becomes lighter, upsetting the whole balance.

How to cheat a scale

The fact

Weight of an object on Earth is the force with which the Earth pulls it towards itself due to gravity.

What you need

- A household weighing machine

How to do the experiment?

1. Stand on the machine as you usually do.
2. Stretch out your hands before you and bend your knees quickly.
3. As you stand on the machine, raise your hands rapidly.
4. Watch what the scale indicates in both cases.

What will happen?

When you bend your knees the scale shows a smaller weight and when you raise your hands a greater one.

Conclusion

As you squat, for a moment your body is in a state of freefall, in which it has no weight. As a result, the scale shows a decreased weight. As you lift your hands, they 'rest' on the body a little more, and a slight increase in weight can be seen.

How to make a rainbow

The fact

We always marvel at a rainbow's colours, we usually see after a shower of rain. But it is possible to make a rainbow even without rain! Let us see how.

What will happen?

A rainbow will be seen on the paper.

What you need

- A glass
- A piece of cardboard with a very thin (1 millimetre) slit
- White paper
- Water

How to do the experiment?

1. Fill the glass with water and place it on the paper.
2. Lean the cardboard against the glass with the slit in a vertical position.
3. Turn the two towards the sun.

Conclusion

The water acts as a prism which breaks down the sun's light into the colours of the rainbow.

21

GENERAL SCIENCE

A mini-cinema

The fact

The human eye tends to retain the image of an object for a short time even after the object has been removed. The image persists for about one sixteenth of a second. Hence, if more than 16 images are flashed within one second, the human eye fuses one image into the other and the impression of movement is formed. Let us see how.

What you need

- Cardboard
- Paper strips with drawings showing a moving object
- Scissors

How to do the experiment?

1. Make two parallel slits on the cardboard. Make sure the distance between the slits equals the size of the drawings.
2. Now pass the strip of picture through the slits as shown in the picture.
3. Pull the strip through the slits quickly.

What will happen?

The figures in the drawing will appear to be moving!

Conclusion

The illusion is formed by the slowness of the human eye, which retains an image for a short time after it disappears. The successive images fuse into one another and an impression of movement is formed.

22

Kaleidoscope

The fact

Plane mirrors are used for many devices, one of which is a toy—a kaleidoscope, which is an interesting device which will give you hours of fun. Its popular name is a children's cinema. Let's see how to make one.

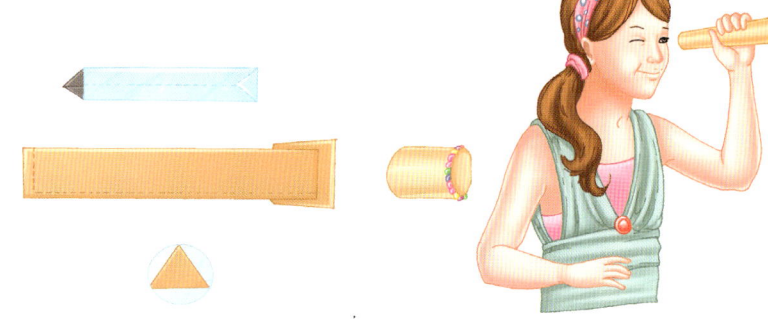

What you need

- A cardboard tube
- Cardboard
- Three long and identical pieces of mirror or plane glass
- Small bits of glass in different colours
- Thick transparent PVC foil or cellophane
- Adhesive tape
- Scissors

How to do the experiment?

1. Tape the mirror (glass) pieces so as to make a three-sided prism (1).
2. Make a circular cardboard cover (2) and tape it to one end of the prism.
3. Insert the prism into the tube.
4. Tape the transparent foil on to the other end of the tube (4)
5. Make a shorter cardboard tube slightly wider than the first one and then also tape foil over it (5).
6. Place a dozen pieces of glass into the second tube, slide it over the narrower tube and seal with tape so the glass pieces are free to move around.
7. Point the kaleidoscope towards a light source, look through the viewing hole (2), and slowly rotate the Kaleidoscope.

What will happen?

You will see beautiful patterns that will change constantly as you turn the kaleidoscope.

Conclusion

The glass pieces are reflected many times in the three mirrors, forming symmetrical patterns.

GENERAL SCIENCE

Misled by water

The fact

When light enters from one medium to another, it bends and changes its way. This is known as refraction. Let us see how.

What you need

- Two large glass tumblers
- One smaller glass
- Three spoons
- Water

How to do the experiment?

1. Fill the glasses with water.
2. Position them as shown in the picture.
3. Place a spoon in each as shown.

What will happen?

The spoon handles can be seen in their normal positions, but those parts seen through the water look magnified and broken, while you can see two spoons in the smaller glass! It looks as if one spoon has been moved from the bigger glass into the smaller one!

Conclusion

The refraction of light makes the spoons look broken. The water in the glass acts as a lens and makes those parts of the spoons which are inside it look bigger. Since the surface of separation, which in this case is the glass tumbler, is curved, the refraction of light makes the spoons look bigger than they actually are.

Refraction can also make an object appear to be in a different position to what it really is. In this case, refraction causes the image of the spoon in the left-hand-side large glass to be formed in the smaller glass.

Water as a lens

The fact

When rays of light pass from water to air, they change direction. In other words, the rays get refracted. Refraction across a curved surface leads to the formation of an enlarged image.

What will happen?

The image of the house when viewed through the jar will appear bigger, as if you are looking at it through a magnifying glass.

What you need

- A drawing of a house
- A transparent glass jar
- Water

How to do the experiment?

1. Tell someone to hold the drawing upright behind the jar which you have filled with water.
2. Move the drawing until the image appears sharp.
3. Look at the image of the house through the jar directly.

Conclusion

Due to its spherical shape, the water in the jar acts as a convex lens and forms a magnified image of the house.

GENERAL SCIENCE

A Balancing Caper

The fact

If you want to keep your body in a state of balance, its centre of gravity and your contact with the ground must be on the same vertical line. This rule can be tested in the following ways.

How to do the experiment?

1. Stand up straight with your back against a wall. Without bending your knees, try to pick up a pencil from the floor. Can you do it?
2. Sit on a chair with your back straight and your legs bent at the knees at right angles. Now try to get up without leaning forward or without tucking your feet under the chair. Can you do it? No matter how much you try, you will not be able to do it.

What will happen?

Here is why you are not able to perform the desired movements. As you sit in the chair, the vertical line passing through your centre of gravity passes through the floor somewhere between the chair legs. When you try to get up, the support is shifted to your feet and your centre of gravity isn't above them, so you lose your balance and fall back in the chair. This explanation is applicable to the first situation also.

Conclusion

When you bend over, your balancing point moves forward. To keep your balance you have to move your feet forward too. The balancing point of an object is called its centre of gravity.

Push at a distance

The fact

Like poles of magnets repel each other whereas opposite poles attract. Let us see how.

How to do the experiment?

1. Fix the bar magnet on the lorry with the help of the sticky tape.
2. Use the other magnet to draw the lorry towards it, as shown in the picture.

What you need

- Two bar magnets with opposite poles
- A toy lorry
- A sticky tape

What will happen?

When you bring the same poles closer, you push the lorry away. When you bring the opposite pole closer to the lorry, you pull it towards yourself.

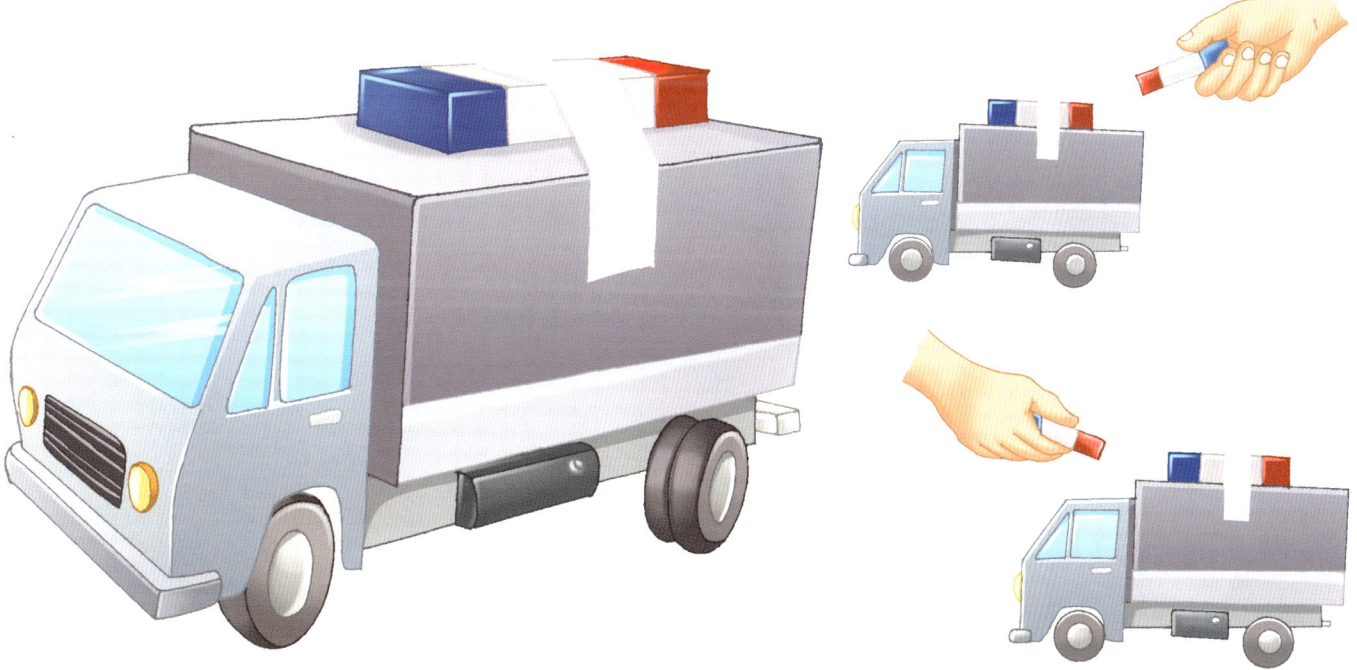

Conclusion

The movement of the lorry is determined by the magnetic force. Opposite poles of the magnets attract each other and hence the magnets are pulled closer while like or similar poles repel each other and are pushed apart.

GENERAL SCIENCE

Energy changes

The fact

Energy can neither be created nor destroyed during the course of a physical or a chemical change. It can only be transformed from one form to another.

What you need

- A broad rubber band.

How to do the experiment?

1. Stretch the band between two fingers.
2. Touch your forehead with the band.
3. Now stretch it out and quickly touch your forehead with it.

What will happen?

The second time around the band will feel warmer.

Conclusion

When you stretch out the band you move its molecules further apart, whereby they gain so-called elastic potential energy. As you release the tension, the molecules return to their original positions, but the energy used is not lost; it is transformed into heat energy. This experiment proves the validity of the rule that energy can neither be created nor destroyed.

Self-adhesive ice

The fact

It is possible to melt ice even without applying heat; pressure can also melt ice.

What you need

- A bottle with a wide neck
- A piece of ice
- Thin metal wire
- Two weights (heavy objects)

How to do the experiment?

1. Place the ice on top of the bottle.
2. Put the wire across the ice and tie the weights to the ends of the wire.

What will happen?

The wire will gradually cut its way through the ice.

A step further

Place two flat pieces of ice on top of each other with a piece of wood and a heavy object on top. Two or three minutes later take off the wood and the weight and try to separate the two pieces of ice. It will not be easy! The reason is the same as in the former experiment.

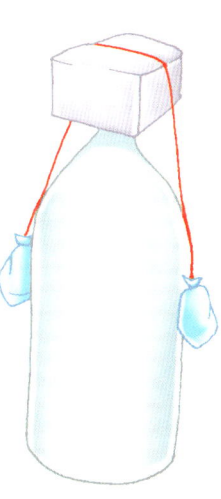

Conclusion

The pressure exerted by the wire on the ice causes friction and an increase in the wire's temperature. The warmed wire then melts the ice and passes through it. The water formed by this process re-freezes very soon and the piece of ice looks completely intact!

The jumping coin

The fact

Air and other gases expand easily when heated. How can we show the expansion of air?

What you need

- An empty glass
- Bottle with a flat top
- A metal coin

How to do the experiment?

1. Moisten the coin with water.
2. Place it on top of the bottle so that air cannot pass by it.
3. Hold the bottle in your hands for a short period of time. Ensure that your palms cover the bottle completely.

What will happen?

The coin will begin to rise and fall, as if it was jumping.

Conclusion

The warmth of your hands is transferred to the bottle as heat, and from the bottle also to the air in it. The air expands, and exerts pressure and therefore also a force on the coin. The experiment is even easier to perform if you immerse the bottle into hot water or hold it over a hot cooker plate.

A step further

Experiment 1

Take two bottles and close their mouths with rubber membranes with some string. Put one of the bottles next to a source of heat (a radiator, the kitchen cooker) and the other into the refrigerator. On the first bottle the membrane will soon bulge out (air expands when it is heated), and on the second it will be sucked into the bottle as the air has been cooled and has contracted.

Experiment 2

Take a pane of glass and raise one side of it on some support. Moisten the edge of a tumbler well and put it on the pane upside-down.

Put a burning candle close to the edge of the tumbler. Soon the tumbler will slip away from the flame. The air in the tumbler will expand and try to escape, but wont be able to do so on account of the water between the tumbler and the pane of glass. The pressure of the heated air will move the tumbler, which will slip, as the layer of water between the tumbler and the glass reduces the friction.

Did you know?

Soil is a mixture of dead plants, animals and tiny pieces of broken rocks. Soils maybe sandy, chalky or clayey.

Index

A
absorption 12
aerodynamic paradox 9

B
bases 7
bicarbonate of soda 5, 7

C
capillaries 12
centre of gravity 13, 14, 26
chemical change 28

E
equilibrium 13, 14

F
fire-extinguishers 5
flavin 7
friction 29, 31

I
inertia 17

K
kaleidoscope 23

L
litmus 7

M
magnified 24, 25
magnifying glass 25
measurement 18
molecules 4, 11, 28

P
prism 21, 23

R
refraction 8, 24, 25

S
spherical 25
surface tension 11
symmetrical 23

T
temperatures 4